american lullaby

american lullaby

Poems by ROBERT A. B. SAWYER

19 Agost 2015

My Dear Herbert,
A pleasure
spending some time
with you. In Return
Enjoy with my Compliments.

Exits but no Escapes Press
New York 2014

Printed in the United States of America at McNally Jackson Books, 52 Prince Street, New York, NY 10012.

ISBN 978-1-941-96922-9

First Edition

Interior and cover design by Patti Capaldi

To CharlotteRusse, my Editor-in-Chief,
without whom this book would not exist
nor life be so sweet.

PLEASE NOTE: the poems "How I Know She's Coming Home" was first published in *Meridian: Best New Poets 2007*; "Fallen (On Broadway)" appeared in *Margie: The Journal of American Poetry, Volume 5/2006*; "Hong Kong Harbor" appeared in *The Nation* magazine, November 13, 2006; "Night in Hell Revisited" appeared in *Margie: The Journal of American Poetry, Volume 4/2005*; "American Lullaby" and "Donald Sawyer's Dead" appeared in *Margie: The Journal of American Poetry, Volume 3/2004*. "Enameled Twilight" appeared in *The Nation* magazine, May 2003, and "Daniel Pearl Got His Story" was included in program of the 2003 "Discovery"/ *The Nation Poetry Competition*; "The Hunt" in *Jazz 2, Jazz Press* 1977.

TABLE OF CONTENTS

Margie 3/04
Nation 5/03

Margie 5/06

Margie 3/04

Handwritten annotations: Meridian Best Poets 2007 (next to line 35); Mangie 4/2005 (next to lines 37–38); Jazz Press '77 (next to line 43); Nation w/ob, Nation 2003 (next to lines 69–70)

AMERICAN LULLABY

1

There is no such thing as barrels of oil. No heavy crude
Drowning the world, no saccharin lighter grades so sweet
They drive mild men wild.
Go to bed my darling, there is no such thing as barrels of oil.
There are only cars made of chrome and polish, flash and speed.
One for every man, woman and child
Who dreams of the open road.

2

There is no such thing as global warming.
Or for that matter old growth forests
Whose canopies could shelter a hundred, a thousand Statues of Liberty.
There is no such thing as habitat loss or endangered species
The world is good and unchanging, my child.
In our forests and lakes and mountains and deserts
Is life beyond counting and reason.

3

There is no such thing as war
No ancient hatreds or blood at the boiling point.
We're one world, whole and indivisible.
So sleep tight in your own soft bed.
And every morning awake in your own bright room.
There has always been enough for everyone
And you will never be asked to do without.

ENAMELED TWILIGHT

This place, so real, it appears artificial
Like the painted backdrop
Of some Technicolor musical
Where real was simply not good enough.
Here too are colors too true—
Blue without a drop
Of anything that isn't blue.

The sky, sapphire
And the gently rolling spaces
Enameled with a hard ice shell
The blue of a weak gas flame.

These trees too are blue.
Bereft of song and sway
They tremble against a transparent sky
Like hands reaching for a moment
More of life.

The park's enameled.
Above it, nothing flies,
Across it, nothing moves
Except for this polished ribboned path
And my own darting brown eyes.

THE DOORKNOB

A hand on a doorknob works like the mind of a detective
At the moment the final clue clicks into place.

The hand approaches the doorknob with the certainty
A detective recognizes the damning, incontrovertible fact.

The doorknob simply waits for the touch of the hand
As the evidence remains in the place it has always occupied.

The doorknob is the perfect expression of fate.
It does not spin like a wheel of fortune, it simply waits.

The doorknob, like the button it so closely resembles, is entirely neutral
It neither beckons nor repels, it has no volition of its own.

The hand that is drawn to it, the hand instructed by some affinity.
Nowhere is this relationship so clear as in our dreams or at the moment of our death.

We die, and the hand, with no assistance from the eyes, no memory to inform it,
Reaches out, takes hold of the doorknob, and turns it to the right.

A LITTLE DAMAGE OR TRAGEDIES NOT AVERTED

1 1998

A poem inspired by the times.
The New York Times.
A poem concerned with a war that wasn't a war.
About a little damage, a few dead.
The dead belonging to the other side.
It starts with a line out of the story.
A grocer named Abdul Gesan speaks:
"Compared with what I saw as a soldier
In the war with Iran and then in Kuwait,
This attack was no more frightening than rain."

"No more frightening than rain."
I read these words a dozen times
They were as subtle and pleasing as haiku.
Now, I want to write a poem about another war that isn't a war
About killing that isn't killing.
But how will I find words
As fine as those spoken by Mr. Gesan.

2 2004

The world is still on fire:
Bloody chaos in Iraq
Palestinians and Israelis at each other's throats
Massacres in Sudan
Madness in the Congo.
No one knows what is happening in Columbia
Or in most of the former Soviet Union.
The best my people can do is hope
Nothing bloody stains what's theirs
Again.

I'd like to forget everything I've ever heard about land mines
In Angola, starvation in North Korea.
And, something regarding 20,000 dead in Eritrea
Who died, I think, for pride.
The contested land was itself brittle and bleached as bone.
I wish I had the courage to ignore the news
Or had the luck to open a page and read about a treaty honored
A peace that held, or tragedy averted.

NOCTURN 1

Disfigured by dark, day's
Inexhaustible colors withdraw.
The growls of traffic sink
into the street
like a man into a woman.

The woman beside me
trembles in her sleep
as night proceeds
like a huge, black barge
up a swollen, moonlit river.

BROADWAY NOCTURNE

Everything he desires man gives himself.
Everything
From inviolate truths seduced
From their inviolate sanctuaries,
To the impossibly pure pelts of children.

Everything.

He denies himself nothing.
The harmless, loathsome, the Quixotic
It's all the same to him.

Everything.

Even the moon
Fractured and imperfect
He took and abandoned
Like a woman in wartime
(And no one was in least surprised).

Everything.

Ugly as he is
Afraid of his own shadow.
Still, he is almost a god.
What could I have been thinking?
Imagine,
It took almost 50 years
Before I knew enough to praise him.

A VISIT TO THE MEMORIAL TO THE MURDERED JEWS IN EUROPE, BERLIN, APRIL 2012

1

If I kill myself tonight
Blame Peter Eissenman, architect, assassin,
My blood on his hands.

The site of his stones, arranged as stones are in nature
Or by our nature—contrived for maximum effect
Gray as a northern January sky.

My heart is a stone commemorating nothing.

2

One may stay on the surface, on the "Field of Stelae,"
Among 2,711 concrete blocks or, if so inclined,
Descend into the museum.

There, privileged as Dante, guided as Dante,
Down into interiors arranged to set
The damned and their victims,
Eternally, face to face.

My heart is a stone commemorating nothing.

3

Am I reading too much into this arrangement?
This all too orderly juxtaposition of the dead
And those who killed.
Those who survived and those who failed
To fulfill their duty.

My heart is a stone commemorating nothing.

4

In the end, to find the words we need, we turn to stone
And we, in turn, are turned to stone.
The silence of stones is the silence of poems.

My heart is a stone that commemorates nothing.

DEATH OF THE SPANISH AMBASSADOR

1

After a ten-minute lull, the fourteen
Year-old civil war resumed
Taking the life of Petro Manuel de Aristegui,
Spanish Ambassador to Lebanon.

On page one of *The New York Times*
Is a photograph of the late Ambassador's living room.
Waist-high in rubble, it looks very much
Like one of our own rural homes
Once the floodwater had receded.

Off to the side, nearly out of the picture,
Is Aristegui's Lebanese bodyguard.
Hands on hips, head bowed,
Not unlike a dog,
That's been caught
In the garbage again.

It is this man who interests me.
This ordinary Joe, in ordinary clothes,
Who could have just returned from the Jersey Shore
Or from buying tires at Sears.

It is this man who compels me to look.
This man who, despite his colossal incompetence,
In spite of enduring fourteen years of war,
And not withstanding the fact in the last week
Another 200 of his people were killed
Has found the time to part his hair
And have his pants pressed.

It is this man I want to know better.
This man whose shoulders shrug so easily
And who seems to know better than most
There's always someone with a broom
Waiting in the next room.

2

In the back of the room, in a niche in the wall,
Intact as a platitude,
Is what looks like a Chinese vase.
There I suspect to remind us that come
What may, the worse always wear itself out
Before it can finish the job.
Or is it that it's always darkest before the dawn
Spills out like laughter?

And it's in this spirit that the *Times* notes
The passing into oblivion of Tilting
Petro Manuel de Aristegui
Who died so he could return a metaphor.
And it's in this same spirit that I dedicate this poem
To his anonymous Pancho Sanchez.
A man who stood so full of life,
In the wreckage of his employer's home,
I could feel nothing but admiration for him.

FALLEN (ON BROADWAY)

I wish I understood the beauty
in leaves falling. To whom
are we beautiful as we go?
David Ignatow. "Three In Transition"

Will I end up like him, oblivious to time and place
Furiously scratching at a small square of paper?
Better him than the woman squatting between parked cars.
Or like that tiny man, who having misplaced everything else,
Decided his shoes were dispensable too.

It's hard to be part of another's fall.
Fall is the only word for it.
Even from a distance it's unnerving. Isn't it?
And aren't we ashamed of our response to it?
How we wish they'd go away, bad dreams and all.

Still, it's hard to see so many falling.
Hard to imagine how anyone can be so alone
Here in a world that sings of little else but love.

FALLEN 2

A man on fire
A woman shrunken as a dying cat.
A child beating his arms like a bird.
"Cockadoddledo."

They emerge like hornets from behind a wall.
Each one inhuman.
Each one more monstrous than the last.

I could say, "Isn't it just like a pageant?"
But we both know better than that.
Only a fool sees beauty in them.
Only a liar sings their praise.

Can a person really be transparent
Or a woman turn to stone?
When a people are exhausted
Anything is possible.
Watch as one man spontaneously combusts
While another blossoms into allegory.

DOOMSDAY
For Ted Getzel

Should sidewalks suddenly buck and bolt
And the City come tumbling down, or
Whether we vanish in poisoned vapor
Or toast in a fireball
If this October wind is the last
To rock my paper lanterns
And this red maple is the last red maple
So be it.

What we had was good enough for me.

When we no longer exist
On that day we cease to matter
The very river we ignored
Will continue to twist toward that same sea
We had long ago crossed and as quickly forgotten.

WHEN MY NUMBER IS CALLED

When my number is called
I will ask for a seat at hunger's right hand
I will bring him his soap and tin whistle.

I will sit by his window
And scowl at his neighbors.
Sit all day and scowl.

Until it's time to wake him
Hand him his coat and open the door
As he steps out to tend his orchard.

FOG IN THE BLACK PINES
AT C. KUSHNER'S IN EAST HAMPTON

Everyone I know has given up
Or lost their faith,
Or renounced their dreams,
And grown indifferent,
In a hundred different ways,
To everything but their symptoms.

We just can't get over being alone.
No matter what precautions we take:
When we need to hear, there's only silence.
When we need to touch, there's no one there.
Awake, long past midnight,
I step out to watch the fog.

Watching the fog roll in is like observing the pieces
Of an accident come together.
You see, but can't prevent, the imminent disaster.
Not that it matters one way or another
What we do or why we do it.
Irrelevance has become part of our fate
There's nothing more to it.
We've been dulled by necessity
And so dully stand by,
As the inevitable — it is always "The Inevitable" —
Determines what will be.
And what will be is always regrettable.

Things — laws, beliefs, even appearances — change
Without bothering to apologize or explain.
A new magician assumes the place of the last
And with a flourish pulls from his hat
A little more of this, a little less of that.

Until even the most rebellious insist
It's simply foolishness to resist.
And so each in turn blanches and falls
To the most popular illusion of all
The one that leaves us in laughter and in tears
By proving we were right to fear
Everything that's far and everything that's near.

DONALD SAWYER'S DEAD OR THE LAST OF
THE GRAY FLANNELED MEN
Buffalo Bill's defunct. e.e. cummings

Margie
3/04

Donald Sawyer's dead.
Who used to stay at the Hilton, Sheraton, Palace, Plaza, St. Regis
And ate at the Palm, Sparks, Gallagher's, 21 and The Four Seasons.
Who wore worsted, twill and gabardine in solids
Pinstripes, glen plaid and herringbone.

The man liked blondes, brunettes and redheads
Tall slender church-going women
Exotic voluptuaries who charged by the hour.
Housewife, coed, salesgirl, brand manager
Chic or raw, it was all the same to him.

He dreamed and kept his dreams to himself.

The man worked, built, gambled, won, lost, began again
And again made it and again threw it away.
He sang for his supper, picked a few pockets
Boasted, bragged, betrayed, and betrayed
In the end, alone, paid the devil his due.

Donald Sawyer's dead
Who walked in Church's, Florsheim, Gucci and Bally
Who flew on PanAm, Delta, American and United
And drove a red Triumph, a black
Lincoln, a white Mercedes, and, when I saw him last,
A borrowed sapphire Jaguar.

He dreamed and kept his dreams to himself.

BUDDHA PICTURESQUE

Great noble heads and fragments of heads
Torsos too
And fragments of torsos.
Every piece holy
From severed hands plump as pigeons
To expansive noses inhaling the perfume of Nirvana.

Why go on?
Because they went on, so I went on
To an arm buried to its wrist
To a head set in a nimbus of roots
Each refusing to comment on its predicament.
For example, why it was left behind while others were
Removed to an apartment on Fifth Avenue
Or around the Parc Monceau.

Some heads are arranged in rows like chessmen.
Arms and legs stacked like cords of wood.
A few odd pieces were set flush against a wall
That was only a memory of a wall.
A few black goats completed the tableau.

Begun at Ayuthaya outside Bangkok

AUTUMN POEM

1

One frigid night
has all but extinguished
an entire season of color.
Abandoned maples and oaks
mark the field like letters scrawled
across a tattered page.

2

At winter's approach flags
of foliage are lowered.
The tattered bodies of maples and oaks
Scrawl across the landscape,
submissive as letters
scribbled in haste.

THE THREE GORGES OF THE YANGTZE RIVER

Dynasty after dynasty after dynasty
From Xia and Tang to the Maoist and Yuan
Poets have praised these rocks
And the fierce river that made them.
But poets are indolent and avoid hard work.

To them a river is a metaphor
Wrecked ships and drowned fishermen are metaphors.
The tears of wives and mothers are beautiful.
Their desperate cries make a kind of music
Which in poems is frequently described as beautiful.

But from this point on, there will be no music.
No more metaphors or, for that matter, poets.
Qutang, Wuxia and Xiling will disappear
Behind the monstrous Three Gorges Dam.
And the water, for all its centuries of howling, will be calm.

"No music," perhaps I've overstated my case.
Metaphors, like energy, won't be destroyed, only transformed.
As for beauty, we shouldn't be surprised when poets find it
In displaced people, drowned villages, engineered landscapes.
After all, what possible use is there in suffering except
To inspire words so full of feeling that they sing.

ROME, ITALY

Old stone
On old stone
On old bone.

A NIGHT AT THE HOTEL CHELSEA

They're gone
And left no forwarding address
But they're the reason I've come.

What I hoped would happen never happened.
That one stayed behind, biding his time, keeping watch.
I would sit and watch him watch me.
Sit while he twirled his stained fedora
'Round n 'round.
Watch him, watch me, making damn sure
He wasn't about to waste good breath,
Before saying:
"Boy, this is how it's done."

Isn't that how the torch is passed
Feeble hand to firmer one
Like the signet ring in a fairy tale?
Isn't that how a link is forged?
But only a draught whistled
Down the halls of this famous hotel.
Here in this empty city
Where what we're paid
Is seldom what we've earned.

HATEFUL AS IT SOUNDS

1

You, me
All of us
Expendable.
As for tears? You
Can always try.

2

Some lives are tragic
Lived entirely in pain
Others, so comfortable,
They eat strawberries
Out of season.

3

You, me
The best of us—
Who hasn't looked in the mirror
Only to fall back in horror
At the face staring back at him?

APRIL RAIN
For Jody Lister

Even asleep she manages to make her way
Quietly intensely as if searching for incriminating letters.
Looking up and seeing no one
I know it's time to go to her.
To put aside the investment banking brochure
That will pay next month's rent.
To forget until morning
Mergers and acquisitions,
Leveraged buyouts and divestitures,
And listen instead to the rain
That's been falling all night.

I want to wake her
Lead her to the window and show her
A rain that is more than weather
That is something rare
Arguably miraculous,
Like an eclipse
Or a hatching egg.

I go to her and watch her shoulders
Rise and fall as if lifted by waves.
Trolling her own waters, she has drifted
Too far out to hear my voice.

Again, I have waited too long.
Let another opportunity come and go.
The rain has stopped and the street reappears
Cars emerge from the dark like rocks from the tide.
Now there is nothing to do but wait.
Wait, listen and watch for her return
Dripping, glistening, to learn what
Of the marvelous passed in the night.

MUSE 1

This is our place
Inhabited and abandoned by lovers
Inhabited and abandoned by dreamers
Inhabited and abandoned by artists
Each and everyone a fool.

We shall live here
Away from everyone else
As if we were lovers
As if we were dreamers
As if we were artists.

You imperious
You inviolate
You relentless
I'll have no other.

Me the embodiment of perfection
Me so impossibly beautiful
Me the last hope of humanity
You my mirror image.

I am the moment of truth.

You are the new day.

But it's been a month since I've kissed you.
It's been a month since I've touched breasts.
It's been a month since I've seen your cunt.

Have you forgotten we were to set the world on fire?

WINTER 2003

1

Do you know what I love about snow?
You can't possibly we've never met.
But I will tell you now on the off chance we will one day.
It's the quiet and how it brings everything to a stop—
Traffic, people about their business, even birds in flight.
For the shortest moment it's as if we all agreed to draw our curtains
And from behind them, count to one hundred.
And then just as quickly life begins again
The way music starts from a music box.
In a restaurant, a woman is leaning away as the waiter places her soup.
At another table a basket of bread is put down, followed by a small plate of butter.
The sounds of silverware scratching plates can be heard from the sidewalk.

2

Who doesn't love snow when it's falling?
When the first flake lands on the back of your neck
And then, when another touches your forehead,
Causing you to look up and watch it fill the air.
Rain is fraught with purpose
Wind hurries back and forth like an obsessive-compulsive;
The sun tells its old stories over and over again
But snow.
Snow purrs like a woman brushing her hair.
Snow chatters like children.
It has begun to snow although not one flake has touched the ground.
The air holds snow in deep and secret pockets.
Tomorrow when I awake and look down on my neighbors' roofs
Down in their yards, there will be a thin layer of snow.
And, if I watch long enough,
I will see it rise like a cake
Made entirely of icing.

GIRL IN A CHOCOLATE SHOP
Ile Saint Louis, May 2004

She's unhappy
And, in a chocolate shop, too.
Of course
One shrugs.
Irony is pretty much the order of the day.
Still one wonders
Why?
A broken nail?
An impatient customer?
Or has she grown bored with chocolate
As one tires of too keen a lover.

She takes a length of ribbon, pulls it as long as her arm
She ties a bow.
I like to think that when she hands off the box
She smiles.
Those expensive chocolates will make someone happy.
This girl could play Lepareto to some Don Giovanni.
Certainly a reward waits in heaven for people
Who water a budding romance
Hasten a reconciliation.
I hope, she doesn't end her day with a piece of toast
A bowl of condensed soup.

I watch her
Stretch
Another length of blue ribbon
Tie another bow.
Still unhappy.
Was another customer rude?
Who would blaspheme the gods
By showing impatience in a chocolate shop?
Then again it's possible
She's grown to detest the scent of chocolate
As they say prostitutes tire of flesh.
Or is it simply that being trapped inside a candy store
Is too unbearable to endure
Like having your cake and eating it too.

SPEAKING OF LOVE
For Charlotte B.

Do not envy me or covet it.
There is nothing erotic in my unhappiness.
There's no moon on fire
No riderless black horse galloping through the woods.
No clock shattered into a hundred pieces.

So why do you insist on coming?
Is it words, more words to misinterpret?
Are you looking for a heart that fits in your hands?
Or do you simply desire a wooden body
To knock knock against yours.

We don't sing out our pain like birds in their cages.
This pain is my pain not your pain.
This dark is my dark.
And that howling that you found so touching last night
Won't be silenced by a kiss however expert or sincere.

HEART

1

Its surface:
Black as asphalt.

Its entrance:
Barred by a crimson velvet rope.

Its voice:
Blah blah. Blah blah. Blah blah.

2

A most ordinary organ.
Yet, it teaches the blind to see.
Yet, it tracks the steps of the most discreet.
And, most astonishing of all,
It even extract music from hunger.

3

So cultured, so tactful, so perverse
I could obey its every command if only
I knew why it insists I stand naked
Before everything I love.

NO DITTY DITTY

I had hoped to leisure and green
but drawn and exposed
I thin instead
and dry toward hollow.

Cornered
brittled, yet it hammers
hammers, hammers away.
I don't know why.

Inching
I crisis
I quiver.

Ink or shout?
I don't know.
Dig, burrow, dig deeper.

A LITTLE NOTHING

When I was a child
A thing was a thing
And that was the interesting thing.

A chair was a chair
Not the idea of a chair
And a bird was that thing with wings.

When I was child
Far away was a mile
And distance an interesting thing.
I'd find in the yard
A path to the stars
And a track around Saturn's rings.

When I was a child
A thing that ran wild
I was the interesting thing.

I'd climb tall trees
And spy through their leaves
A boy high above all other things.

THE DEAD END AT THE OPEN ROAD

Afoot and light-hearted I take to the open road ...
Walt Whitman. "Song of the Open Road"

On the Open Road I stumbled on an appalling truth:
How street lamps, no less than stars,
Provide all the illumination
Anyone will ever need.

There I learned to keep unhappy thoughts to myself
And instead accentuate the positive and
Accept with a smile what's offered:
Four walls, regular meals
The occasional press of flesh.

If you find yourself on the Open Road, desire little
Expect nothing
And learn to love without shame
The monsters that keep us whole
And our enclosures from rupturing.

THE MORE THINGS WE MISS, THE MORE DREAMS WE HAVE

"The War Diaries" by A.G.
In the August 1999 issue of *Harper's* Magazine.

I don't want to dream
I want much more—
Expensive watches, fountain pens and good things to eat
Including fresh fruit out of season.

The fact is, Mr. A.G., I'm rich
And give myself everything I want
The most understanding women, seats in the orchestra
Paris in the spring.

So while it may be true that I am doomed
To sink into sleep like a man fallen overboard:
No dreams, no music, a heart still
As a stack of coins, lungs flat as a newspaper.
I must confess my indifference to dreaming.

Beauty, Mr. A.G., real beauty, resides only in things
And happiness, in the possession of them.
Everything else is a delusion, a lie that pretends
We don't prefer our reflection in the mirror
To a field of poppies, or a starry night.

The problem with dreaming is that it's incompatible
With the purpose of our hands.
These elegant, if covetous, appendages
Exist to offer, yes, but first to take and to hold.

That they are attracted to the brightness of cherries, the heat of flesh
The snap of paper money
Is not their fault.
They are, after all, only the slaves of our eyes
Organs which are beside the point in the dark.

MY LIFE RUNS FROM ME TO YOU LIKE A SPOOKED HORSE

1

The world is ice.
The world is thorn.
It doesn't matter how often you ask
No one will ever love you
The way you want to be loved.

2

They won't, not for a moment,
Put down their forks. Won't
Lean on their shovels
Or hang up the phone,
No matter how beautifully you sigh.

3

The days turn over, one by one,
Like the cards in a game of stud poker.
Hands, cock, hair.
One is closed.
One is limp.
The other thins.

4

Wind, moon. heart.
One you can't see.
One is vain as pastry.
The last is hollow, hollow, hollow.

5

Enamored with the rough edges of the world
I dream of friction and of the sparks
That fly from your flesh
When it's scraping mine.

I'VE TOLD NOTHING BUT LIES MY ENTIRE LIFE

When it's late ~~you~~ and you're alone you come back
To the original version:
A bright morning. Birds in the trees. Signs
Everyone reads as propitious. Then,
The loving family steps off to one side
And a young man learns
What it means to be alone in the world.
With a grin, a wave, he sets off,
And before he knows it arrives where it will begin.
Not afraid to sweat or bleed or love a little
He will, at the right moment, find the treasure he sought
Under the bed he made himself.
That's how it goes in a thousand tales.
But it is not my story.
It is simply an old story
The one I adopted once my failure
Began to make a regular spectacle of itself.
Ancient disappointments at home,
Forgotten humiliations in the classroom
On the ball field, between the sheets
Long ago written off as inconsequential
Find their way back into the narrative.
For its part, the city was everything
Novels and guidebooks promised.
But the truth is always something else.
Something more
Something less.
The truth: I've been lost for the better part of 20 years.
Now, all four points of the compass
Are as worthless as a clock without hands.
I've told nothing but lies my entire life
And now it's too late to stop.

INORDINATE PRAISE OF A WARM RENTED ROOM
ON A WET NOVEMBER NIGHT

What I want I find
Inside these walls,
Behind this door.
All I want I have:
A descent
A silence
That not so much defies speech
As perfects it.

Outside rain slashes
A voice flares and dies
As suddenly as a struck match.
While inside, all around me,
The electric pulse of
Invisible machinery
Keeps the imperfect peace
Of modern life.

All is requited.
I am warm when it is cold.
Dry when it is wet.
Yet it has come to this:
My ascribing human qualities to
Thermostats.
Still, this is what it always comes to:
A man dreams of solitude
Only to find himself
Describing the involuntary dance of meters
As a shuddering of sorts.

HOW I KNOW SHE'S COMING HOME
For Jodi Lister

Her apricot soap French milled and expensive
Is wrapped in violet tissue paper
And hidden in the medicine cabinet.
In the dish on the sink she left behind
A bar of Ivory.

Plain and substantial as a baseball
That's for me.
Five thousand miles away
And she does not want me to use her soap.

I unwrap it and hold it as carefully
As an antique netsuke. Its perfume
Rises like a summer morning
Reaching through a screen door.

When she's here I receive strict instruction
Not to use her creams, shampoos or powders.
Although I may touch any part of her body I please
Her beauty products are taboo.

Yesterday, it removed bus exhaust and sweat
Leaving her face soft and damp,
So when I kissed her it was like touching moss.

Today, I run water, make a lather and inhale.
Although it's my face that looks back from the mirror
It is her scent that slips into the room
Like a secret hushed from the lips that held it.

GOOD NIGHT

To find His light
I made my own dark.
Although I'd been assured
It was extinguished some time ago.

I continue on.

I move through my dark
By touch, by smell, by instinct
By fear, by hurt, by doubt
By bruise, by cry, by blood.

I continue on.

The universe expands or contracts
Its entirety contained on a black board
Marked by white scratches.

I continue on.

I am not discouraged that the sun sets
Or by that same treacherous sun's return.
Light, dark, dark, light, neither illumines or conceals my way.

I continue on.

NIGHT IN HELL REVISITED

He had never seen God, but, once or twice,
he believes he has heard Him. W.H. Auden

1

God continues to seek us in the strangest places.
His eyes lit from within
Like pearls in their gray closets.

2

He still calls out in that hoarse whisper of his
From those alleys he prefers
The ones with no way out.

3

When we pray, He appears
Shimmering in wavelengths invisible to the eyes He gave us
And in frequencies unintelligible to our famous brains.

IN A CHURCH BY CHANCE

I am so tired of being observed
Of holding my tongue
And hiding my nakedness.

I've seen enough.
I've heard enough.
I've endured too much.

But before I go tell me.
Why are bright objects
Never bright enough?

CONTAINERS

1

That things must be contained is a sign of their inherent instability. As Yeats observed some time ago, life is predisposed to "come undone." Undone, unbuttoned, discarded, that's just how it is, in spite of our best efforts. Bags, baskets and boxes are filled only to be emptied of their contents. Lids, seals, screw tops of varying ingenuity will unfailingly fail. Even the body, perhaps the most ingenious of all containers, is not impregnable. Once the spirit is called, it will leave its shell vacant, adding it to the piles of waste left behind. That things are intended to unravel, that our strongest adhesives and latches will prove inadequate to the job, should in no way discourage our desire to contain everything there is to contain.

I've a 50-years-old penny in my wallet. Although minted the year I was born, there is no reason to believe it won't outlive me. I may lose it before I myself am lost, or it may be recalled in a great government-sponsored copper drive, but I prefer to think that it will survive at least as long as the 2,000-year-old Roman coin I also keep in my wallet for luck. What is certain is that while the penny will likely remain physically intact, it is just as likely that its original meaning will be lost. Which is, of course, just another way of saying: This penny will be pitched.

Yes, every treasure, including those hearts we cherish, will be dust and so swept up and removed somewhere. Boredom, global warming, a collision with an asteroid, these and 10,000 other fingers will empty even our most tightly sealed containers. Which is how it should be. A match unlit is worthless. A toothbrush sealed in its plastic sheath will not fight a single cavity.

2

Giovanni's daughter Sophia is allowed to run freely through the Bar Pitti. She visits the regular customers who all adore her and she makes new friends as she dashes table to table. She does not appear to be contained until her mother calls out, "Sophia eat something. Sophia, come eat your macaroni." So, I see, I am mistaken; she is contained, even if by something as limitless as a mother's love.

POETRY, LOVE AND LOSS

You
sitting there
all ears.
Me
with 1,000 fewer words
than yesterday.

THE HUNT

In the distance twilight builds a bridge
Dark marches
There is no mistake
A deer nibbles the silence between the petals of an apple blossom
Is disturbed by snapping branches
And an instant of flame lights his eyes
Startled the deer strains for an understanding
And steps up a hill undulating toward infinity.
Ears and tail erect it remembers
Silence and a cool wind calms.

A man with a gun squats his mouth fills with chalk.
Understanding flowers in his head as
Blossoms fill the basket of the deer's stomach.

The deer moves with ease among the trees
Behind him the expanse of night yawns
The deer has seen the man
Who stands points the gun and holds his breath
The deer as if suspended on a watchchain listens
The flames extinguished are two black pearls
That reflect the sad fury of twilight.

Here is the fraternity desire
The deer knowing rises on its hind legs
To savor the last blossom.

At the stroke of acquiescence is peace
As life relaxes its hold
Struggle lies down and surrenders its teeth.

The man fires and a roar resounds through the orchard
Hurling the man to a dungeon of bells
The deer turns faces the man and for an instant
God is present in the distance between
The bullet and the skull.

ON OUR LAST VISIT
In Memory of BH

What long bones he had and in the end
He was all bone.
Behind closed lids small hard bones
Perhaps if he could not see death
It could not see him.

Death was in the room.
But Burke would not be hurried.
He waited as bones grew out of his sleeves and
Up through the neck of his sweater.
Out the bottom of his pants stretched cool slender bones.

"Is this it?" he whispered,
He guessed correctly.
When he had nothing more to add
That's when he reached out
Five long boney fingers
To take the hand of the original Mr. Bones.

THE SPIRIT BEGINS TO LEAK

One day the spirit begins to leak and we
Wither and find we tear, all too easily.
While the baubles
We received for our troubles fizzle and pop.
We are left no more than shell
With years of dust left to gather.

Those we love darken too
His, her decline and ours in step
Which is not lovely to watch
But we do watch.
There's nothing to be done. I'm afraid.

IN THE JAPANESE GARDEN, PORTLAND, OREGON

A leaf trembles at the end of a twig
And a poem of James Wright comes to mind.*
The poet is staying at a friend's farm
He's lying in a hammock
Observing the play of light on bark and leaf
As the sun sets.

Perhaps the others have gone to town
Or are in the kitchen preparing dinner.
Suspended between heaven and earth
The man confides to us: "I've wasted my life."
Counting one less leaf clinging to this dwarf maple
I know exactly how he felt.

* "Lying In A Hammock At William Duffy's Farm In Pine Island"

INTERSECTION

What happiness there is in crowds.

Where else do we feel so alive
As when we must maneuver, push and force
Our way around more men and women and children
Than we've ever conceived possible in a single place?
All of who have come for the same reason we have:
To find themselves immersed among their own.
What a delight it is to be among our own.

What happiness there is in crowds.

In losing one's self, while knowing it is impossible to ever be lost.
Here din is music, music as profane as it is sacred.
If there is light it illuminates nothing and illumines everything.
If it is dark the dark is absolute and conceals no one
How wonderful it is to be among men and women and children
Who, having found this place, have also discovered
No crowd is impenetrable
And every dream is habitable.

What happiness there is in crowds.

JUST COMPLAINTS

1

Somewhere a man no better than me
is writing the poems
I was meant to write.
The cool ones
that bring shivers
down the long, taunting backs of women.

2

I am a long way from my handsome youth.
No one here persists:
"You, I love you.
The world is many
but it is you alone
Who I love."

LALIQUE WINDOWS IN THE COTY BUILDING ON 5TH AVENUE

It was 1912 and beauty mattered.
A window could be transformed.
From something to look through
Into something one looked at.

Toward that end, Rene LaLique went to work:
A three-story composition in glass.
Poppies and vines, climbing skyward.

Today, it is merely a historical footnote: Art Nouveau
A quaint idealization of nature.
When was the last time you heard the word, quaint?

The work was lost, decades passed, and then, by accident, found
Although no was looking for it.
Then, just as suddenly, it was lost again.

DEAD DEER ON MUIR DRIVE

Deer do not comprehend
the scrambled Braille of asphalt
and this one, dragged
to the side of the road,
had read with feet that stammered.

Where the fender had opened
the worn leather case
tendon and muscle twisted
taut and dry as twine.

Twilight, the last of light
And this broken beast will not see the dawn
And I've no words to assure it
It will arrive after this darkest night.

LEGACY

We die with empty hands
That was your final lesson.

You might have taught:
We live with empty hands.
But that would have been too abstract
A gesture. Instead,

You wished me every bright object, everything
Sweet, everything ripe, but left nothing
Having lost everything
You accumulated over 80-odd years.

You should have told me:
We expand, contract, and in the end
Have nothing to show for our pain
But our pain.

Now, a year after your death,
I am no closer to understanding how things are lost
Or why it is necessary
We must lose them.

SENSE OF PLACE

So few places are truly habitable
And those, always in the possession of others.
For the rest of us, it is a matter of occupying space.
While the home we envision, green and enviable,
Is always just around the bend
Waiting beneath a sun that throws its gold
Like an oriental potentate.

The place where we receive our mail
With its address raised on our tongues
Like the letters on a license plate
Seems so unreal, a place
Where others might at any time intrude
Stand where we stand
Take from us the key that opens the door.

When we finally consent to settle
And sink our roots
Among old kitchen smells,
We don't find the peace we imagined.
Not in the fieldstone house
With its descending carpets of lawn.
Nor in the pied-à-terre with its crablike
Hold on the clouds.
For no roof can withstand the menace that resides
Behind the elastic, transparent, leaky shell
That passes for our heaven.

LAUGHTER

Out of scrambled knots,
chinks and loose ends, the idea
of my failure took flight.
Rowdy as a gull
it swooped, dashed, shot
beyond my reach. Beyond
my fist, stone, curse
it hovered and laughed.
Laughed until my heart,
tumbling down winter's corridor,
deflated like a beggar
at the gate of a tower.

MOON FROM THE CORNER OF CHARLTON AND 6TH AVENUE, SEPTEMBER 19, 2002

Ladies and Gentlemen, I direct your attention overhead.
Ladies and Gentlemen, I present to you a marvel.
Ladies and Gentlemen, I give you your moon.

Are there no takers?
No one among you who will steal a glance?
Ladies and Gentlemen, I implore you.

What has she done to be so reviled?
This spent coin.
Shorn collaborator.
Empty promise.

Ladies and Gentlemen, I offer for your pleasure
Ladies and Gentlemen, step right up and see for yourself
Ladies and Gentlemen, for one night only

This broken heart.
This downcast eye.
This frozen tear.

Ladies and Gentlemen, there's nothing to fear.
Look into this blind mirror
And see yourself as you really are
More than a fragment but less than whole.

THE MOON OVER WASHINGTON SQUARE PARK

1

Gibbous,
but who knows that word today?
Say instead, "Homely blur, sagging breast."
Moon, I don't know how to praise you.
Why should I
when there's no money in it?

2

Look,
the moon
is snared in a tangle of branches.
Its delicate light, caught and held,
like some marvelous beast
trapped by ordinary men.

FIRST SPRING POEM, MARCH 23, 1988

It's winter in the *Times* but in Central Park
The surface of the boat pond flashes
Light and silver as applause.
Although their limbs still scrape and saw
Trees are noisy with birds that only yesterday were gone.
Joggers run bare legged. One woman's thighs
Are pink as coral.

In spite of all of this, some people wear heavy coats
Buttoned to their throats.
They blow into their hands and hurry by.
It takes time to shed and thaw.
Time to believe that spring,
Like the lover, whose betrayal was winter itself
Is back and whispering through the door.

HUDSON RIVER

1

It is bitter but you come.
Is it this tug straining up river?

2

The river swims beneath a faceless sky.
Its frozen banks run along without a sound.

3

There is so much you want to say.
What a pity no one will ever hear it.

ORANGE BLOSSOM

"[Avro Pärt] took a pen out of his pocket and put it in front of me, as if that would explain everything. 'Schubert's pen,' he said, 'was fifty percent ink, fifty percent tears.'" The conclusion of Alex Ross' Profile of the composer Avro Pärt, "Consolations" in *The New Yorker*.

1

What would our lives be like if such things were possible?
If pens wrote with tears and when you kissed your lover
You tasted a mouth full of orange blossom.

How different the world would be if when you made love
The bed was surf and foam, salt and spray.
What if you could compare her to a summer day?
But the world is not castanets, falling stars, blood oranges.
It is fissures and cracks and things that snap in your hands.

2

The lone gunman
The woman who drowns her child
The child who wanders into traffic
Why do we insist such acts are inexplicable?
(Unkind, yes. Inexplicable, no.)

Why do we do these things and worse?
Because we know, know too well
We will never write with a pen that's fifty percent ink
Fifty percent tears
And will never, ever,
Not if we live to be a hundred
Taste a mouth full of orange blossom.

POTIONS, ELIXIRS, PROMISES
For Charlotte B

They are arranged as bottles often are
In small clusters, or like chess pieces in disarray.
Often they're placed at eye level
And set in descending order
Or in ascending order
Like children in a family portrait.

If there are labels, they tend toward fancy
And their names printed in fonts that wander
From the baroque to the laboratory.
French, or a kind of French, seemed to be the preferred language
Used to tell their lies.

Unlike prescription and patent medicines they are left in the open
Perhaps because they possess a kindness—even the haughty ones—
Bright faces for the faces they nurture and flatter.

But they can also stand serious, medicinal and measured.
Glass and resins smooth, long limbed and proud
These are the ones that elicit knowing smiles:
No, time won't be slowed by the richest cream,
Or distracted by essences captured one night each year
In a land very ancient and very far away.

THE ORIGINS OF SPEECH

When rivers roared and gods
On mountaintops grumbled
Defiant nature was
To black ignorance wed.
Then, through ash and dung,
Man crawled.
Rain sick, wind sick, sea sick,
Huddled and far flung
Over pocked-marked earth
Stone piling, rag fastening
Man.

Things spoke then.
So many mouths.
And man, starving or feasting,
Under stone, thatch, beam or sky
Squatted, trembled and
Listened.

There was life in things.
Spirits
In the air.
Women in water.
And always, everywhere
Hunger
Spewing like an engine
Improvising
Speech.

CYRANO IS BORED

Never again will I perform
death-defying acts
Only to accept as my due
a
single
Grape.

Never will I swallow
another
sword
For my supper.

The pen is dry at last
Tra la la la la la.

I want nothing more to do
with anything that suggests
resembles
Or goes by the name
Mr. Panache.

I have reached the end of my metaphors.
And not even the shimmer
of her divine flesh
will elicit another superlative
from
me.

Welcome to my silent new world
where monuments are tall as inches
and
planets
round
as
minutes.

THE TRIUMPH OF THE MARKET

I want bottles, glass bottles.
Bottles clear as dawn in December
Opaque as the bottom of the sea.
Slender, delicate bottles that bring to mind a young girl's wrist
And brutish glass, blunt as the working end of a hammer.
I want bottles that sing when tapped with a fork
Or, when blown into by a child, bellow like creatures chained in Tartarus.

All these bottles exist and many more beside.
Bottles filled with perfume, honey, even mother's milk.
Bottles concealing poisons so cruel their venom pushes against the glass
Like an assassin removing his knife from its sheath.

I want bottles that are topped by cork stripped from trees in Portugal.
I want bottles corked by synthetics, cut and colored to resemble cork.
I want bottles with screw tops and bottles that open at the urging of a church key.
I want bottles that collect in basements dressed in the dust of decades.

I want the bottles that Morandi fabricated in the glassworks of his mind.
I want bottles saloon brawlers in TV Westerns broke on the heads
Of greenhorns, and bottles that fit so snug in the mitts of poolroom thugs
They might be extensions of their bloody fists.

I am not ashamed to admit I also want among my collection
Bottles used to perform unnatural acts in blue movies, stag films and other
Cinematic displays of depravity.
These bottles are wonders to behold.
No less than the one perfect example of the craft,
The original Chanel #5,
Which mirrors the ideal proportions of the Place Vendome,

You may ask whether my desires fall within the respectable limits
Of the collector's whim
Or believe they wander to the edge of eccentricity, and perhaps cross
Into the shadow land of the mad.
What does it matter?
As what cannot be questioned is objects exist capable of containing both
The curbside effervescence of seltzer and the sparkling constellations
Poured at creation from a cosmic bottle of Dom Perignon.

Do I alone admit to this compulsion?
Look, across 6th Avenue, poking through the garbage with a stick
An ancient Chinese woman.
On the pavement beside her
A broomstick with a plastic bag tied to each end.
And, what fills those bags?
Cans, yes, but what brings an emerald flame to her eyes?
The discovery of a bottle, the one that hides in its unimagined depths
The dredges of immortality.

TROMPE L'OEUIL

Walls
Everywhere.
Locked doors.
Shuttered windows.

What is to be done?
What does it matter?

Everything that appears
And everything that refuses
Does so by permission of the artist.

IMPERFECTION. A WORK IN PROGRESS.

1

The body is imperfect.
Every day it finds new ways
To tell us this
So we'll never forget.

The mind is imperfect.
Every day it conducts new experiments
To demonstrate this fact
So we'll never forget.

The soul no one has ever seen.

2

Everything that's ever existed
Everything that exists today
And everything to come
Imperfect.

3

Why then do my eyes open
If all is destined to dust and dark?
And, why take her hand
If she, too, is simply passing through?

WINTER WALK NO.1, 1995

These trees, stripped bare.
I feel so embarrassed for them.
Is it because I also know what it's like
To extend an empty hand?

NEW SNOW, NEW YEAR 1988

Fragrant as a book opened for the first time
the sky is the faintest blue
imaginable
and sharp as cut glass.
Six a.m. and only bits of frozen snow
stir on West 77th Street.

Everything else, all the familiar
desired and feared
facts of life
are at this moment
inexplicably
absent.

Here in the stillness
amidst the emerging
it is possible to believe
in an absolute good.
To believe if these naked trees had mouths
they too would sing.

TWILIGHT TURNING

Gulls fly up the Hudson.
The sun takes back its light.
Leaves snap under foot.
A face on the street looks familiar.
Everything we watch stands still for us.

HONG KONG HARBOR 1984

On this side of the window
A shower of chrysanthemum.
Outside, torrential rain.

From this distance the world appears mute.
But if somewhere someone is singing
It's because someone somewhere is listening.

If this were the last day of my life, would I know it?
And if I did
Would I pretend otherwise?

DANIEL PEARL GOT HIS STORY

What is conceived and shaped and held by light
What comes to life in the light
These things don't exist in the dark.

The dark isn't what you think.
Or what you imagine in the light
The dark to be.

I wanted to illuminate the dark
And see for myself its different heart.
And give it a voice.

I assumed such tricks could be turned.
I was wrong.
The dark can't be penetrated by light.
You can not know the dark without living in the dark.

pause

A LIFE IN BRIEF

A Boy's Life

1

The day in its leisure dragged a stick across
The whale ribs of a picket fence.
Doors flung open, slammed shut
And a thousand balls flew and fell.

The boy grew into a man never suspecting how his absence
Grew beside him.

One day was like every other stacked blue on blue.
The sun's butter poured over the glistening streets.
The boy's appetite was enormous
He tasted the sweetness all day.

He was a brimming and nicked hands that fastened on anything bright.
As he rode a red bicycle to the park
Across town, his absence directed traffic around him.
It mowed lawns, pruned hedges along the way.

Later, after the game was won and dusk fell
Over the field, his absence sat in the dugout.
Wind whistled over bleachers
As through a ruined barn.

2

Tucked in bed with starched white sheets
Pulled taut over his head,
The boy slept to dream.
Great was the night.

Great was the jungle he found there and
The boy knew the way in, into the trembling sleeve of black.

The boy did not have to see the gloriously feathered birds
To know they were there.
Nor feel the hot breath of a stalking leopard to know
It was right over him.

Crashing through the dense canopy thrashing and uprooting;
Driving apes to despair and birds to slap the air
With enraged wings was his father's bark.
His mother, not timid, growled back.

Two wild dogs encircled each other.
Teeth bared, snarling.
"Whore."
"Bastard."

Then came the slap,
The shot,
That sent monkeys
Into their panicked frenzies.

Under the camouflage of his blankets, the boy furiously dismantled
The innocent workings of his grandfather's watch.
The shiny wheels, levers and springs,
He laid out, like the tiniest collection of bones.

3

The sun rattled the window.
Pings of light, bright as tropical fish,
Darted from under the shade.
No one had to call the boy twice.

He awoke as if he never slept.
As if sleep was just a mother's invention.

It was summer, a boy's glory.
Long days and the hills that began
Where the painted lawns ended
And ran all the way to the ocean.

That day he and a friend would rediscover forgotten Indian trails
That led back to the old west.
They would seek stolen gold protected by pumas
Rattlesnakes, scorpions, and crazy men escaped from asylums.

While the boy drank his milk pouring strength into his bones
As he laced up his boots and put water into his canteen
His absence climbed the street, up the slowly warming asphalt.
Up as the shade gave way to hard white light.

Along the way mothers stood at front doors
One hand holding robes closed at the neck, the other high in the air.
While their men turned their backs on beds still warm
To enter a world without women or children.

A Man's Life

1

One day the boy vanished and in his place
Stood a man.
Suddenly a man and for the first time
Completely alone.

The boy had owned his world, the man was forever uncertain.
Stuck in that impossible situation— a boy commanded
By his mother to leave the room and ordered by his father to stay
Exactly where he is.

What was this sudden ambivalence?
Wife, children, money, so many things to weigh
But everything was flashing water
Racing past his hands.

2

Like a prisoner the man carries inside his head
A perfect model of his cell.
Fist tight
Infinitely expanding.

Like a fugitive the man avoids the sharp eyes of each day
Like the pensioner he grows feeble
Watching the iron of his labors shed, flake and trail
smoke.

The boy loved his friends hated his enemies.
What he feared deserved to be feared:
The roiling black surf of night, the stranger's long sedan
Idling tense as a Doberman Pinscher.

But the terrors that stalk a man were different:
Daylight receding like a hairline, the splintering laughter of women

The boy never noticed his absence.
He was his world and the world was his.
The man saw his absence everywhere.
And everyday.

Still the man denied it.
This is what makes the man a man:
Denying the knowledge he's acquired.
Knowledge burned into him as if drawn by rope.

So after framing diplomas,
Pocketing bonuses and persuading a woman to love only him
He merely endures the passing time of day.
Hurting as only flesh can.

Enduring time: to the concentric whirling of planets,
To the hammering of acceptable passions,
To the ceaseless rain of processed
Forms and cancelled checks.

3

There is only the man, the man and his absence waking,
Washing, shaving, dressing,
Walking, standing, shitting
Waiting and waiting.

The Man Waits

1

The man waits: on street corners,
In corner bars, behind the wheel
Of his automobile—
Drumming his fingers.

He waits for nothing in particular. No one
In particular.
Just as he looks for nothing
In particular in the bloodshot eye of a sunset,
On the endlessly copulating waves,
In the polished faces of women.

He simply waits as one waits in a doorway
For a break in the rain.

2

Every man, every one of us knows an abandoned gas station
There on a strip just outside of town, surrounded by dried weeds.
Its candy-colored stripes fading.
Its enamel signage loose, slapping at air.

Everyone of us American men knows an abandoned storefront
Waiting for fire to rid its stench of failure and impotence.

3

Everyone of us.
Every mother's son of us waits.
Dragging on cigarettes,
Loitering with newspapers, waits.

Or staring down TV sets, telephones and monitors
Waits
Between the legs of our women.
Waits

Waits for the cry to burst out, for the boy
To cartwheel back to life.

4

Waiting the man looks at his hands and asks, "What happened?"
Just as the boy once studied a dead sparrow.
His hands trembling, fretting.
His mind not grasping
What in the world happened, or why?

ACKNOWLEDGEMENTS

"As a poet, I write for the good opinion of two hundred people in this country." Poet, Editor, Publisher George Hitchcock in *Durak, The International Magazine of Poetry, No. 1.*

American Lullaby would not exist without the love, support, encouragement, skepticism of many, too many, to acknowledge here, but a few who must be mentioned, including: Family: my grandparents, the late Murray & Elsie Schneiderman; my mother, Dolores Anthis; my father, the late Donald Sawyer; my brother, Brett Sawyer & his wife Eliza; & my brother, the late Charles Sawyer; my sister, Kirsten Sawyer Abdo; my stepmothers, Patricia Phelps & Jan Sawyer; my father-in-law, the late John Barnard.

My patron and irreplaceable friend Ken Simon, & his wife, Marinette Simon.

Friends and relations who who don't need to be reminded of the nature of their contribution to *American Lullaby* include: Peter Arnell; Kathleen Baum; Constantin & Laurene Boym; David & Elaine Brandt; Matthew Buccheri; Neke Carson, Richard & Nardyne Cattani; Eric Chen; Andrew & Kay Conn; William Cooperman & David Hubley; Matthew Courtney; Eyal Danieli; Daniel D'Amelio; Alexander Davidis; Michel Delsol; Giorgio DeLuca; Alfred & Christiane Divorne; Steven G. Eckhaus; Joe Fox; Marty (Limbo) & Elaine Freedman; Nina Gapinski; Stacie & Damien Gray; Terry & John Giordano; Howard Goldberg; Bob Greenberg; Rainer Gross; James B. Hall; Peter Haratonik; Linda Hattendorf; Kevin, Shaunice, Ymani & Kalvary Hawkins; Fayette Hickox; Ted Hilton; the late George Hitchcock & Marjorie Simon; Julianne Holland; Minnie Hickman; Pamela Burlingham Hurd; Mary James; William Kochi; Dr. Stephen & Cynthia Krigsman; Cedric Kushner; Melissa Olds Lavitan; Jodi Lister; David Masello; Lisa Maxwell; Robert McDowell; the late Jimmy Mirikitani; Anita Monteith; Anna Moore; John Murphy; Thomas B. Murphy, Jr.; Soos Packard; Janice Page; Andrei Petrov; Murray Peek; Joseph & Anne Pierson; William, Polia & Boris Pillin; Emily Prager; Paul Rich; the late Alan Roy; Grace Schulman; Andrea Selby; Charles Simic; John B. Simon; the late Steven Sipos; Rev. Jacob Smith; Lavinia Branca Snyder and Brian Snyder; Brad Starks; Ed Stern; Kelli Taylor; John Toland; Natasha Trethewey; Vieri Tucci; Judith Von Hoffman; Caldwell Williams; Michael Weiner; Philip White; David Wong; Frank Yeung; Skot Yobbagy; Carolin Young; Jason Yowell.

Finally to the Doctors who kept me "whole and my enclosures from rupturing." Marianne Burlinger, Mark A. Eberle, M.D.; Gary Evans, DPM; Bert S. Goldfinger, D.D. S.; Samuel L. Guillory, M.D.; Ann Hill, M.D.; Andrew M. Milano, M.D.; Stephen B. Richardson, M.D.; Harold J. Weinberg, M.D.